"This was a really powerful book for me. Alt
working on unhooking from my people-ple
the last six years and have made significant progress, from this
book and workbook I experienced a depth dissolving of my core
beliefs that hadn't happened before. Earley's style of writing
and online system are very concise and elegant. The book flows
smoothly, and the website works well. This is such a neat system,
and I use the tools daily to smooth my way. Thanks for this
magnificent contribution in the form of the Pattern System. It's
truly amazing!"

— Jill Sosna

"To say I am familiar with people-pleasing thoughts and
behaviors is an understatement. I live and breathe them. Even
after years of work on myself and improvement, this pattern still
operates in me. And in my role as therapist, I see this behavior
in my clients daily. This is why I am grateful to Jay Earley for
not only this book but the new series of ebooks, workbooks,
and the online community with a buddy system to support
you while you wrestle with the issues. What I find most helpful
about the book is the directness and practical applicability of this
new format. It goes straight to the heart of the matter and asks
important questions about the subconscious patterns that are
keeping you hooked to pleasing.

I am finding the journey through the online workbook
enlightening, helpful and challenging. I really appreciate Earley's
directness and pointed questioning. I heartily recommend
this book and this approach. I will be using this resource as a
consistent check to monitor my taking care of myself. I will also
use it regularly in my practice to help the many clients who come
to me with people-pleasing struggles. Great work!"

— Josephine Ludwig, RPh, MA, PLPC

"I found this book useful, easy to follow and gentle in its
approach. It has successfully avoided jargon but encouraged
me instead to look for my gains, needs and fears with regard
to my people-pleasing. It offers insights about why we seem so
often to be stuck in unsatisfactory and repetitive behavior. It also
emphasizes the means and choices for change. I liked the layout,
where case examples, graphics and the workbook make for lively
reading. The daily and weekly check-ins kept me engaged."

— Ines Hasenfuss

A Pleaser
No Longer
Becoming Assertive

Jay Earley, PhD

 PATTERN SYSTEM BOOKS
Larkspur, CA

A Pleaser No Longer: Becoming Assertive

▨ PATTERN SYSTEM BOOKS

140 Marina Vista Ave.
Larkspur, CA 94939
415-924-5256
www.patternsystembooks.com

Paperback ISBN-13: 978-0-9855937-3-5
LCCN: 2012947600

Printed in the United States of America

Introduction to the Pattern System Series

This is a series of books that are based on the *Pattern System*[SM]—a comprehensive mapping of the human psyche. You can use the Pattern System to obtain a complete map of your psyche. You will be able to see your strengths and your defenses, your places of pain and how you compensate for them. You'll come to understand the structure of your inner conflicts and see where you are ready to grow. The Pattern System makes clear what you need to explore next in order to resolve the issues that are most important to you.

You'll learn where there is underlying pain, shame, or fear that must be healed. You'll also learn which healthy psychological capacities you can develop (or are already developing) to become happier and more productive.

In the Pattern System, *patterns* represent dysfunctional behaviors that cause problems for us or other people. *Healthy capacities* are the ways we feel and act that make our lives productive, connected, and happy. The Pattern System organizes the patterns and capacities according to various psychological *dimensions,* such as intimacy, power, and self-esteem.

Once you learn the basics of the Pattern System, if you choose to explore more deeply, you'll learn other concepts. At a deeper level are *motivations,* which are the types of intentions underlying your behavior and which are often unconscious. They are derived from the hurtful ways you were treated in childhood, which are represented by *wounds*.

Each book covers one pattern and the corresponding healthy capacity that is needed to break free of it. In the process of learning about each pattern, you can delve into its motivations and the wounds behind them. This will help you to transform your way of living from the pattern to the capacity.

See http://thepatternsystem.wikispaces.com for an outline and fuller description of the Pattern System.

Acknowledgments

I am grateful for detailed and helpful suggestions from Cate Wilson and Bonnie Weiss.

I appreciate the sharp eyes and clear mind of Kira Freed, who provided quality editing as well as interior design for the paperback version. As always, I love the clear aesthetic that Jeannene Langford brings to cover design.

Rachel Whalley created the workbook and provided great ideas for the icons in the Interpersonal Patterns graphic. Charlie Alolkoy drew the icons, and Kira Freed created the exciting graphic. Kathy Wilber has done an excellent job on the programming behind the workbook.

Contents

Introduction

Do you always seem to go along with what other people want? Do you frequently find yourself trying to make other people happy and avoid upsetting them? Do you try to be nice in order to avoid conflict? Are you afraid to assert yourself or set limits when other people are hurting you? Do you feel as though you have to take care of other people's feelings, but no one seems to care about yours? Do you have a hard time saying no when someone asks you to do something?

If you answered yes to some of these questions, you are one of the many people struggling with the People-Pleasing Pattern. Of course, it is a good thing to be kind and helpful to people and make them feel good, but maybe you go overboard in this direction. You may find it hard to speak your mind, to say what you want, to say no, or to advocate for what you believe in. You may find it difficult to even know what you want or feel because you are so focused on other people's needs and feelings.

If you are tired of this pattern and would like to make a change, this book is for you. It will help you understand the fears and needs that are behind your People Pleasing and where they come from in your past. It will help you learn how to become assertive and strong.

This book will help you to have the courage to take a stand, ask for what you want, state your opinions, and speak up when you don't like something. As a result, your needs and thoughts will become just as important as other people's. You will have an equal say in what happens, and people will take you seriously.

This doesn't mean that you will become pushy or demanding. It doesn't mean that you will stop caring about other people and wanting the best for them. However, you won't be doing this from a place of fear or need. When you do care for people and help them to feel good, it will come purely from a loving place in you. And you will also care for yourself and your needs.

You will develop the strength and personal power to get what you want in life while still being a kind and loving person.

The Pattern System and
Internal Family Systems Therapy

This book is primarily based on the Pattern System (see Introduction to the Pattern System Series). Internal Family Systems Therapy (IFS) is an extremely powerful and user-friendly form of psychotherapy that I use and teach. IFS and the Pattern System complement each other. The Pattern System provides a theory of the psychological content of the human psyche, while IFS provides a powerful method for the healing and transformation of psychological problems.

I have chosen to write this book in such a way that you don't need to understand anything about IFS or parts. For those of you who already know IFS, the concepts in this book are completely compatible with it and can enhance your IFS work on yourself. In Chapter 9, I explain how IFS can be helpful in enhancing the work described in this book.

How to Use This Book

You can use this book to explore either your own People-Pleasing Pattern or that of another person. The book is written in terms of the reader's pattern, but you can easily apply what you learn to other people. Chapter 2 is for those of you who are reading this specifically to learn about another person.

Visit http://www.personal-growth-programs.com/ a-pleaser-no-longer-owners to register yourself as an owner of this book, and I will immediately send you an ebook version.[1] As I write subsequent books in this series, I keep

---

1. I will send you a Kindle version, which you can read on your computer, tablet, or smartphone using free software that you can download from Amazon.

noticing improvements I want to make in previous books. If you register as an owner of this book, every time I improve the book, I will email you the latest ebook version. You will also be notified about each new book in the series as it comes out.

Even though this book is a workbook, there is also a workbook on the web at http://www.personalgrowthapplica tion.com/Pattern/PeoplePleasingWorkbook/People_ Pleasing_Workbook.aspx that goes with this book. There are many places in the book where you can check off items or fill in blanks. You have a choice of doing this directly in this book or using the web workbook instead. All the information in the web workbook will be held under your name and password with complete confidentiality and security. At any point, you will be able to return to the web workbook to look at your answers, change them, or print them out. You will be able to use either workbook to engage in the life practice in Chapter 7.

This book is aimed at helping you change. Therefore, it is crucial that you fill out this workbook or the web workbook and do the practice to change your People-Pleasing Pattern.

We are forming a People-Pleasing Online Community of people who are reading this book and would like to support each other in letting go of People Pleasing. You can find the Online Community at http://www.personal-growth-programs.com/connect. We will help you find a buddy to talk with as you are reading the book, and especially to help you engage in the life practice in Chapter 7 and to support you in taking action. You can also participate in discussions and phone meetings where you share your struggles and triumphs with others who are dealing with the same issues around People Pleasing. The meetings and discussions will be facilitated by myself or a colleague, and we will be available to answer questions of yours that come up.

This support could make all the difference in your success at using this book to work through People Pleasing and achieve your goals. It is part of a larger community of people who are working on personal growth and healing through our books, websites, and programs.

Many different patterns are mentioned at various points in this book. Most of these are just for you to explore in more detail if you choose to. If you just want to move ahead to get help with your People-Pleasing Pattern, feel free to ignore these patterns. It isn't important that you remember or understand them. Just keep reading to get the help you want.

I congratulate you on your willingness to embark on this exciting inner journey. You will soon discover how the People-Pleasing Pattern operates, the unconscious motives behind it, and where they likely came from in your childhood. You will discover how to transform this pattern so you can be strong and assertive. You will also explore the various aspects of the Assertiveness Capacity and how to cultivate them. And finally, you will have the opportunity to reclaim your personal power to go with your kindness and caring.

Chapter 1
Your People-Pleasing Pattern

If you have a People-Pleasing Pattern, you have a tendency to over-please people to make them happy. You often try to be who other people want you to be, to agree with them, to fit in. You try to make yourself think, feel, and want the same things as others, even if this doesn't reflect your true feelings.

If you are in a relationship, a part of you may be trying to "merge" with your partner and act the same as they do. If your partner expresses an opinion about a movie you just saw, you automatically agree. If your partner wants to go bike riding rather than hiking, you feel the same way. This process is often unconscious and involves ignoring your own opinions, feelings, and needs, or distorting them so they are almost always the same as your partner's. You just defer to their preferences, values, and goals without quite realizing you are doing it.

It is important to be able to distinguish between situations in which you genuinely agree with your partner and those in which you automatically go along without even considering what you think or want.

If you frequently agree with what other people want and they seldom go along with you, this is an indication that you have the People-Pleasing Pattern. Another indication is if people express frustration that you never seem to come up with ideas or preferences of your own and instead always "follow the herd."

Another more adverse way this pattern can appear is that you go far out of your way to please people and make them happy.

Of course, there is nothing problematic about wanting to make another person happy. However, the problem arises when you do this without even considering what would make you happy, or when you try to please others at your own expense. You might even try to please people when those particular actions end up causing you hardship. There may be special circumstances when it would be a loving gesture to sacrifice your well-being to please someone when they are in serious trouble. And there may be situations in which you choose to go along with someone for strategic reasons, for example, to avoid alienating your boss. However, if you do this frequently, you have a People-Pleasing Pattern.

False Belief of the People-Pleasing Pattern: It is dangerous to assert myself. I must please others for them to like me and connect with me. My needs don't count compared to other people's.

A Story of a People-Pleasing Pattern

When Lauren goes out on a date, her primary concern is, "How much does he like me?" She doesn't bother to ask herself, "Do I really like him?" She doesn't just enjoy herself; rather, her focus is on pleasing him. She tries to figure out what his preferences are, and POOF! They become hers without her even realizing it. If she says something that he seems to disagree with, she immediately backpedals and changes her opinion. No matter what movie or restaurant they go to, she finds that she has roughly the same opinion of it as he does.

She isn't really aware that she is trying to please him—it just sort of happens that way. This sometimes works out in the short run, making a man want to see her more, but over time it backfires. She often comes across as bland and subdued. She's not very interesting to be with because the real Lauren isn't there!

When Lauren is with her friends, she goes out of her way to take care of them and make them happy. She lets them talk about themselves as much as they want and listens with interest and enthusiasm. She only talks about herself if they ask. Some friends rarely ask her about herself, and she ends up feeling used and resentful, but she suppresses this reaction because of her need to please them.

Lauren has been dating Joe for a few months. One day Joe said, "I need to talk to you about your behavior around my family."

"What's the problem?" Lauren replied, showing deep concern.

"Well," he frowned, "we see them a lot, and I wonder if you could be a little more outgoing and friendly with them."

Lauren immediately felt bad and tried to figure out how to give Joe what he wanted. She never even considered whether or not his demands were reasonable. She didn't ask herself, "How friendly am I actually being with his family?" or "How do I relate to them?" and "What is Joe really concerned about?" She didn't consider the possibility that Joe and his family were making unreasonable demands of her to be a certain way. Her only thought was: "How can I comply with his request? How can I get him to stop being upset with me?"

However, Lauren didn't experience it as a request, but rather as a demand. This is because she expected other people to control her and run her life. She tried to remember to be more "cheery" around Joe's family, but she hadn't even figured out what this meant, so it was hard for her to do.

Lauren's story will be continued later in the book.

People-Pleasing Behaviors and Feelings

The following are common behaviors and feelings that come from the People-Pleasing Pattern. Which of these apply to you?

☐ I let other people plan the activities for our spare time.

☐ I often say, "Whatever you would like to do is fine."

☐ My opinions and responses to events usually match those of others.

☐ If I make plans, I try to ensure that other people will like them.

☐ When someone express an opinion, I usually agree without having to think about it much.

☐ It is hard for me to disagree with others.

❐ I follow other people's lead when it comes to interacting with other people.

❐ Sometimes it feels to me as though my partner and I are one person.

❐ I try to be who others want me to be.

❐ I am afraid to rock the boat. It's hard for me to know what I want.

❐ I avoid speaking my mind.

❐ I find it easier to go along with what other people want or with their opinions.

❐ I fantasize about a strong person taking over my life and making it work.

❐ It is difficult for me to say no.

❐ I avoid getting angry.

❐ Other behavior _____

_____

❐ Other feelings _____

_____

If you prefer to use a workbook on the web rather than filling out your answers in this book or on paper, visit http://www.personalgrowthapplication.com/Pattern/ PeoplePleasingWorkbook/People_Pleasing_Workbook_ Behaviors_and_Thoughts.aspx.

You don't have to engage in all these behaviors to have the People-Pleasing Pattern. And for the ones you do have, you don't have to be doing them all the time.

Your People-Pleasing Pattern might be operating all the time, or it might be triggered only under certain circumstances, such as when you're on a date or when a relative asks a favor of you. Think about the circumstances that tend to trigger your People Pleasing.

People-Pleasing Thoughts

If you listen carefully to your thoughts, you may become aware of ones that are related to People Pleasing. Here are some examples. Which ones resonate with you, and in which situations do they tend to come up?

❐ I'm happy that my partner and I are so much alike.

❐ It would be awful if we didn't agree.

❐ I'll just do whatever someone wants.

❐ Even if I feel differently from someone, it isn't worth disagreeing.

❐ Don't make waves.

❐ I'd better make sure my partner or friend is feeling okay.

❐ I need to be careful not to hurt others.

❐ I want everyone to get along.

❐ Try to be nice.

❐ I shouldn't express how I really feel.

❐ Other behavior _____

_____

❐ Other feelings _____

_____

Situations That Trigger People Pleasing

What are typical situations that trigger your People-Pleasing Pattern? In other words, when do you become super accommodating and lose the ability to speak up for yourself? For example, on a date, when family members ask for favors, with a boss who makes unreasonable requests, when someone hurts your feelings? List the situations in which you go into people-pleasing mode. Be very specific— for example, when someone asks your opinion, when a relative or coworker teases you about a tender topic, or when you're invited to an event you don't want to attend. You will process them later in the book.

_____

_____

_____

_____

Types of People-Pleasing Patterns

There are a number of different kinds of People-Pleasing Patterns. Check off the ones that are closest to yours.

❐ Compliance

You go out of your way to make sure that you go along with what other people want and what they think. Most of the time, you don't even consider what you want, which makes it easy to give others what they want. You also don't really consider your own opinions on matters—you just agree with other people, especially those people you are close to and whose approval really matters to you. Your goal is to be what they want you to be, though this may not be conscious.

You often end up relating to people who expect you to comply with their wishes and might be upset with you if you didn't. It is very important to you to avoid upsetting them at all costs.

❐ Merging

There is one special person you are close to, and you try to be the same as this person. You want the two of you to be one, and the way you try to accomplish this is to bend yourself so you are just like them—you want what they want, think like they think, feel what they feel, and so on. This makes you feel deeply connected and safe. Your intention to merge in this way may not be something that you are consciously aware of.[2]

❐ Caretaking

You do your best to take care of other people, especially if they are in pain or if something you might do could cause them pain or discomfort. You always want to be there to nurture and support them, no matter what it costs you. You especially don't want to make them uncomfortable or cause them pain, and you go out of your way to avoid this, even when it goes against your needs or causes you pain.[3]

❐ Conflict-Avoiding

You are frightened of conflict and do your best to avoid it. If someone confronts you or brings up a conflictual issue, you usually just give in to them in order to avoid any difficulties. You immediately take the blame without even considering whether or not you are to blame—anything to end the argument. If someone expresses a strong opinion that differs from yours, you will often change your mind to placate them.

If there is something that is bothering you about a friend's behavior, you avoid bringing it up with them, no matter how uncomfortable it makes you. You may not even

---

2. This is related to the Dependant Pattern (http://www.personal-growth-programs.com/dependent-pattern). Follow this link (and those throughout the rest of the book) to see if the book for this pattern is now available.

3. In this case, you have the Caretaking Pattern (http://www.personal-growth-programs.com/caretaking-pattern) as well as the People-Pleasing Pattern.

let yourself know that it bothers you so you don't feel any conflict about not dealing with it.[4]

❒ Basic Pleasing

You go out of your way to make other people happy, even when it means making yourself unhappy. Your needs and well-being don't count—only those of other people. You give other people the best seat, the best portion of food, and so on. You often make special arrangements to make someone happy.

Of course, there is nothing wrong with wanting the best for people and helping to make them happy, but you often do it at your own expense. Most importantly, you do it out of the fear of not making them happy, or out of a need to get their love or approval, rather than just doing it from a pure place of kindness and love.

Notice that some of these types are related to other patterns, which you might need to explore to work through your People Pleasing. Click on the links on these patterns to see which of those books are available now.

Please don't feel that you have to remember all the different patterns and capacities that are introduced in this book. Just explore the ones that are relevant for you. The Pattern System will gradually make sense the more you use it. To see an overview of the whole system, read Appendix A or visit http://thepatternsystem.wikispaces.com.

As you read about these patterns that you might have (and others later in the book), please don't judge yourself

---

4. In this case, you have the Conflict-Avoiding Pattern (http://www.personal-growth-programs.com/conflict-avoiding-pattern) as well as the People-Pleasing Pattern.

because you may have some of them. We all have a variety of different patterns of relating that don't work for us. There is nothing deficient or wrong with you because you have some—in fact, just the opposite. You are reading this book because you are interested in learning about yourself and changing your patterns. You are to be congratulated for your commitment to self-awareness.

At this point, if you aren't sure whether you have the People-Pleasing Pattern or another pattern related to power, read Chapter 8 and take the quiz on the Power Dimension.

CHAPTER 2

Other People's Patterns

How Your People-Pleasing Pattern
May Affect Other People

You may be attracted to people with a Controlling Pattern[5] because it fits so well with your tendency to comply with other people. However, in the long run, this probably won't work so well unless one or both of you work on changing your patterns. You may eventually get tired of your partner always getting their way. You may resent losing your autonomy and start withdrawing or become passive-aggressive. Or your partner may get tired of your never having any preferences or opinions.

If Someone Close to You Is a People Pleaser

If you suspect that someone close to you has a People-Pleasing Pattern, you may be reading this book to try and

---

5. http://www.personal-growth-programs.com/controlling-pattern

understand his or her behavior and feelings. This can be very helpful in getting clear on where this person is coming from.

In addition, this book can help you understand yourself more deeply. It is possible that you are inadvertently contributing to this person's pleasing by being controlling and demanding. Consider whether or not this might be the case before trying to help this person.

How to Relate to a People Pleaser

If you are close to someone who is a People Pleaser, there are some things you can do to minimize this tendency in them. Try to avoid triggering this person's fears that lead to pleasing. Read Chapter 3 and Chapter 4 to get a sense of which underlying fears this person might have that lead them to be a pleaser. Talk with them to get a better sense of what they might be afraid of. This will help you to be aware of times when you unintentionally trigger this person's fears.

For example, if this person is afraid of being judged or rejected if they don't please you, be on the lookout for anything you might say that contains any hint of criticism or dismissal. Even if this person is overly sensitive to judgment or abandonment, you can maximize the chances of him or her feeling safe with you by watching what you say.

If this person hints that you are being critical or rejecting, stop for a moment to consider what they are saying and see if it is true. See if you can become aware of such behavior in the future so you stop acting it out. You can even make a point of being explicitly accepting and reassuring to this person.

CHAPTER 3

The Underlying Motivation for People Pleasing

Outline of the Change Process

The next five chapters constitute the heart of the change process for People Pleasing. Here is an outline:

- Chapters 3 & 4: Understand underlying motivations (mainly fears) for People Pleasing and their origins in childhood.

- Chapter 5: Work through these fears so your People Pleasing begins to let go.

- Chapter 6: Explore the Assertiveness Capacity that you will develop to replace People Pleasing.

- Chapter 7: Engage in a life practice to make this happen.

Motivations for People Pleasing

In order to change your People-Pleasing Pattern, it is very helpful to understand the underlying motivation behind it and its origins in your childhood.

You may be a People Pleaser because you are afraid of being emotionally harmed or rejected if you stand up for yourself instead of going along with what others want.

Some of your fears might be conscious, but others can be deeply buried. You might even know that there is no real danger if you stop being a People Pleaser, but an unconscious part of you is still afraid of it.

This chapter introduces another concept from the Pattern System. *Motivations* are the underlying reasons behind your patterns—what drives them. Your motivations might involve fears, rebellion, or other intentions.

How to Approach This Information

There is potentially painful material to explore in this chapter and the next one. Take it slowly and make sure that you are OK emotionally. Take a break any time you feel the need. Call a friend to talk about the feelings that are coming up, if that would help you feel supported through this process.

As you read through these motivations and think about the ones that pertain to you, please don't judge yourself. It is common for our Inner Critics to use this information to make us feel bad about ourselves. They tell us that we are really screwed up, that we'll never have love. Don't believe these self-attacks.

Keep in mind that everyone has a host of fears, needs, and other underlying motivations for their behavior. And everyone has had a variety of childhood wounds. We don't all have the same wounds and fears, but we all have plenty of them. It is perfectly normal to have a variety of these issues.

You aren't bad or pathological or inadequate because of the ones you have. If your Inner Critic is beating you up about your fears, let it know that judgment isn't helpful. When you can take in new information from an open place, it helps you to see yourself more clearly.

Adopt an attitude of looking at yourself objectively and compassionately as you explore your motivations and wounds. This approach is enormously helpful in learning about yourself. You had to develop these patterns of defense because of the ways you were wounded when you were very young and vulnerable. They aren't your fault. Appreciate yourself for being interested in delving into this material so you can stop being a People Pleaser.

Motivations

Let's look at the different motivations for being a People Pleaser to see which ones resonate with you. Look over the following to see which ones apply to you. If you aren't sure, read the next chapter for more details about each of these motivations and where they come from in childhood.

Fear of Harm

❏ I am afraid of being yelled at or struck if I don't please people or if I assert myself.

❏ I am afraid of being criticized if I don't please people or if I assert myself.

❏ I am afraid of being shamed if I don't please people or if I assert myself.

Fear of Rejection

❐ I am afraid of being rejected if I don't please people or if I assert myself.

❐ I am afraid of not being cared for or being abandoned if I don't please people or if I assert myself.

❐ I am afraid of being dismissed, discounted, or not valued if I don't please people or if I assert myself.

Attempt to Get Connection

❐ I am trying to get acceptance and interest by pleasing people so I don't feel unlikable.

❐ I am trying to get approval and admiration by pleasing people so I feel good about myself and don't feel deficient.

❐ I am trying to get love by pleasing people so I don't feel unlovable.

❐ I am trying to get caring by pleasing people so I don't feel deprived and abandoned.

Attempt to Stop Harm

❐ I try to stop people from intruding on, smothering, or violating me by pleasing them.

❐ I try to stop people from yelling at or hitting me by pleasing them.

❑ I try to stop people from judging me by pleasing them.

❑ I try to stop people from shaming me by pleasing them.

Powerlessness

❑ I feel powerless and expect other people to run my life.

Belief in Pleasing

❑ I believe it's right to please people.

Being the Opposite of a Parent

❑ My mother (or father) was so aggressive, judgmental, and rejecting of people that it made my life difficult or was embarrassing to me, so I swore that I would never be like that. I went to the opposite extreme and tried to be pleasing to everyone.

The next chapter goes into more detail about each of these motivations and their origins in your childhood situation.

Chapter 4

Details About Motivations and Childhood Origins

For each type of motivation from the previous chapter, there is a section in this chapter with more detail about that motivation and the childhood situation it comes from.

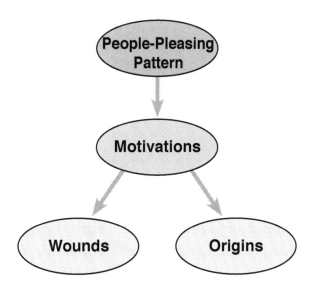

There are a number of different ways to use this chapter.

1. If you already have a pretty good idea about your motivations, you can skip this chapter and perhaps come back to it later to explore where they come from in your childhood.

2. You can go directly to those motivations you checked off in the previous chapter and only explore them.

3. You can read through the entire chapter to get a fuller understanding of your motivations and where they come from. However, if all the detail doesn't feel helpful right now, feel free to skip to the next chapter and come back to this one at a later time.

This chapter introduces two more concepts from the Pattern System. *Wounds* and *origins* are the ways you were treated when you were a child that led to your dysfunctional patterns of behavior as an adult. *Wounds* refer to the pain underlying your motivations, while *origins* refer to the ways your behavior was shaped in childhood.

How to Approach This Material

Caution: There is a lot of detailed and potentially painful material to explore in this chapter. Feel free to stop at any point when you feel you have processed enough for the moment or for today. Take it slowly and make sure that you are OK emotionally. Take a break anytime you feel the need. It often helps to process things gradually. When you sit for a while with something difficult, you can digest it more easily, like a big meal. Call a friend or your buddy from the People-Pleasing Online Community to talk about the feelings that are coming up, if that would help you feel supported through this process.

Many motivations and wounds are named in this chapter. It isn't important that you remember or understand them all—only the ones that are relevant to your People-Pleasing Pattern. Feel free to ignore the others and just focus on understanding where your People Pleasing comes from.

If you have more than one of these motivations and wounds, don't try to process them all at once. Monitor yourself so you can process what you are learning and so you don't get overwhelmed emotionally. Just look at some of them, and come back to the others later.

If two or three of these motivations or wounds seem similar to you, don't worry about teasing them out—just check off all of them. For example, if shame and judgment seem similar to you, it is probably because you were both shamed and judged. Just check off both of them and then, in Chapter 7, process them together.

Now let's begin with the first motivation.

Fear of Harm

You might be afraid of being harmed in some way (for example, criticized, shamed, or yelled at) if you stop People

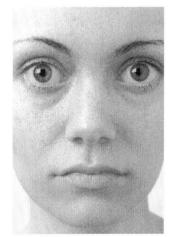

Pleasing and speak your mind. Of course, it is possible that you have been harmed for speaking up, but most likely this fear comes at least partly from your underlying issues.

There are three things you might be afraid of, and each is related to a wound. Look them over to see which one fits your People-Pleasing Pattern. You might have more than one.

❏ Fear of Being Yelled At or Hit

You might be afraid of being yelled at or hit if you don't go along with others or if you stand up for yourself.

This is related to the *Attack Wound.* When you were little, your parents (or others) may have yelled at you because you didn't agree with them or because you spoke up for yourself. They may even have abused you physically for not complying. Now you might be frightened of being treated that way again.

❏ Fear of Being Criticized

You might be afraid of being criticized if you don't go along with others or if you stand up for yourself.

This is related to the *Deficiency Wound.* When you were a child, you may have been criticized and made to feel inadequate for not going along with others. This criticism may have come from your parents, siblings, or someone else you were close to. You might be afraid of this happening again in your adult life.

❏ Fear of Being Shamed

You might be afraid of being shamed if you don't go along with others or if you stand up for yourself.

This is related to the *Shame Wound.* When you were little, you may have been ridiculed, shamed, or embarrassed by parents or others you were close to if you disagreed with them or spoke up for yourself. You might be afraid of this being repeated in your adult life.

Soothing Your Pain

As you read through these descriptions of childhood experiences, painful emotions may come up. It is helpful to soothe yourself when this happens. The best way to do this is to treat each painful emotion as coming from a child part of you, an inner child who was wounded when you were young.

Take a moment to contact this child inside of you. You may see an image of this inner child or feel him or her in your body, or just have a sense of the child. Open your heart to this little being. Be the compassionate, nurturing parent that this wounded inner child needs right now. Listen to his or her pain with caring. Imagine holding this child in your arms. Let the child know that you are there for him or her. Give this inner child the love he or she needs. And give the child whatever else he or she may need.

- Acceptance: "I accept you just the way you are."

- Validation: "You are a good person."

- Encouragement: "You can do it."

- Support: "I am standing behind you 100%."

- Appreciation: "You are very precious to me."

This will keep you from being overwhelmed by the pain that is coming up, and it may even help to heal that wound in you.

To listen to a guided meditation for nurturing this wounded inner child, visit http://www.personalgrowth application.com/Pattern/PeoplePleasingWorkbook/ People_Pleasing_Workbook_Inner_Child_Meditation.aspx.

Fear of Rejection

You might be afraid of being rejected in some way if you don't go along with others or if you stand up for yourself. Of course, it is possible that you have been rejected for speaking up, but most likely this fear comes at least partly from your underlying issues.

There are three major types of rejection in the Pattern System, and each is related to a wound. Look them over to see which one fits your People-Pleasing Pattern. You might have more than one.

❏ Fear of Being Rejected

You may be afraid of being rejected in some way if you don't go along with others or if you stand up for yourself.

This is related to the *Unlovable Wound.* When you were a child, your parents, siblings, or friends may have rejected you when you didn't comply with their wishes, and you ended up feeling unlovable. Now you might fear that happening again.

❏ Fear of Not Being Cared For or Being Abandoned

You might be afraid of not being cared for or being abandoned if you don't go along with others or if you stand up for yourself.

This is related to the *Deprivation Wound.* You may not have gotten the love and care that you needed when you were young, and your parents said or implied that this was because you disagreed with them. Or you may have been abandoned by your parents at a time when you really needed them, and they gave you the impression that it was because you weren't enough like them. They may even have blamed this on something you said that differed from their opinions or values. Now you might be trying to get this love and caring by being overly compliant and keeping a low profile.

❒ **Fear of Being Dismissed, Discounted, or Not Valued**

You may be afraid of being dismissed, discounted, or not valued if you don't go along with others or if you stand up for yourself.

This is related to the *Deficiency Wound*. When you were a child, your opinions and perspectives may have been dismissed and not valued, which may have made you feel inadequate, worthless, or bad about yourself. You might be afraid of this happening again if you speak up for yourself instead of going along with other people.

Attempt to Get Connection

You may be trying to get acceptance, approval, love, or caring by pleasing people. There are four major ways this can happen in the Pattern System, and each is related to a wound. Look them over to see which one fits your People-Pleasing Pattern. You might have more than one.

❒ **Attempt to Get Acceptance and Interest**

You may be trying to get acceptance and interest by People Pleasing and attracting the attention of people who are important to you so you don't feel unlikable or unacceptable.

This is related to the *Unlovable Wound,* which is described above.

❒ **Attempt to Get Approval and Admiration**

You might be trying to get approval and admiration by People Pleasing so you feel good about yourself and don't feel deficient.

This is related to the *Deficiency Wound,* which is described above.

❒ **Attempt to Get Love**

You might be trying to get love by People Pleasing so you don't feel unlovable.

This is related to the *Unlovable Wound,* which is described above.

❒ **Attempt to Get Caring**

You might be trying to get caring by People Pleasing so you don't feel deprived and abandoned.

This is related to the *Deprivation Wound,* which is described above.

Attempt to Stop Harm

You might be trying to stop people from attacking, judging, shaming, or intruding on you by pleasing them. Of course, it is possible that you have been harmed in one of these ways, but most likely this fear comes at least partly from your underlying issues.

There are four major ways this can happen in the Pattern System, and each is related to a wound. Look them over to see which one fits your People-Pleasing Pattern. You might have more than one.

❒ **Attempt to Stop People from**
Intruding on, Smothering, or Violating

You might be trying to stop people from intruding on, smothering, or violating you by People Pleasing.

This is related to the *Violation Wound.* Your parents (or someone else) may have smothered you emotionally or intruded on you in a bodily way. For example, they may have forced food on you or even abused you sexually. Now you might be afraid of being violated again if you draw attention to yourself by disagreeing or being outspoken.

❏ **Attempt to Stop People from Yelling at or Hitting**

You might be trying to stop people from yelling at or hitting you by People Pleasing.

This is related to the *Attack Wound,* which is described above.

❏ **Attempt to Stop People from Judging**

You might be trying to stop people from judging you by People Pleasing.

This is related to the *Deficiency Wound,* which is described above.

❏ **Attempt to Stop People from Shaming**

You might be trying to stop people from shaming you by People Pleasing.

This is related to the *Shame Wound,* which is described above.

Powerlessness

You may feel powerless and expect other people to run your life.

This comes from the *Domination Wound.* You may have been dominated and controlled by one of your parents, and you were powerless to do anything about it. Now you might expect to be dominated and powerless in your current relationships, too.

Belief in Pleasing

You may believe that it is right to be pleasing to people. There are five possible origins that could contribute to this belief.

Modeling Origin. One of your parents may have been a People Pleaser, so you grew up assuming that that is the way a person should be.

Teaching Origin. Your parents may have told you how important it was to please people and take care of them, so you came to believe that that is the way a person should be.

Reward Origin. Your parents may have rewarded you with praise whenever you pleased them, so you came to believe that that is the way a person should be.

Punishment Origin. Your parents may have punished you when you didn't please them, so you felt that you had to be pleasing in order to be safe.

Shaping Origin. Your need to be pleasing may have been shaped by your childhood, which involved a combination of modeling, teaching, punishment, and/or reward.

Being the Opposite of a Parent

Your mother (or father) may have been so aggressive and controlling that it made your life difficult or embarrassed you, so you swore that you would never be like that. You may have gone to the opposite extreme by People Pleasing.

Next Step

Whew! All of this chapter may have been hard to read. Yet it was necessary in order to come to an understanding of what motivates your People Pleasing and where this tendency comes from in your past. This will be helpful in changing this pattern.

You should now have a pretty good idea of your motivations for People Pleasing. Take your time and get emotional support to process these insights. It can be a lot to take on.

You are now prepared to change your People-Pleasing behavior, which starts in the next chapter.

CHAPTER 5

Working Through People-Pleasing Fears and Motivations

Now that you know which of your underlying fears are pushing you to please people, let's work them through so you can be assertive when you want.

When you are with a particular person or in a certain situation, your People-Pleasing Pattern may become activated. This pattern developed in childhood because you were dealing with a harmful situation, for example, being judged or yelled at, or because your needs weren't met unless you were pleasing. And unconsciously, you believe that this is going to happen again.

However, your current situation is very different from what

happened back then. You are no longer vulnerable and dependent like a child. You are autonomous and no longer subject to the power of your parents. You have many strengths and capacities now as an adult (and possibly because of previous work you have done on yourself) that you didn't have as a child.

For example, you may be more grounded and centered. You may be able to assert yourself, be perceptive about interpersonal situations, support yourself financially, and so on. You have already accomplished many things in your life  and overcome various obstacles. You are an adult with much greater ability to handle yourself. You probably have friends, maybe a spouse or lover, perhaps a community you belong to, a support group, professionals you can rely on. You have people you can turn to if necessary.

This means that you aren't in danger the way you were as a child, and your mature self is available, which wasn't possible when you were young. Therefore, it isn't really necessary for you to people please any longer because this is a reaction to the past hurts and dangers.

In this chapter, you can work through the fears that lead to People Pleasing. You can do this for any particular person or situation that leads to People Pleasing. Choose one specific situation and apply the rest of this chapter to it. Then when you are finished with that situation, if you want, you can come back to this chapter and choose a different situation to process. I will call this the *Life Situation* for the chapter.

Are Your Fears Realistic?

First we will consider whether or not your fears or perceptions are accurate. Are the things you are afraid will happen if you aren't pleasing really likely to happen? For example, if you are afraid of being judged if you don't please someone, consider whether this person would really judge you. If you are afraid of not getting acceptance or approval from someone unless you please them, consider whether or not this person might appreciate you anyway.

These questions aren't always easy to answer without bias. Consider them when you aren't emotionally triggered. Keep in mind that even though there may be a part of you that believes you will be harmed or rejected, this may not actually be the case. You might want to discuss this question with friends who know your situation.

If Your Fear Isn't Realistic

If you decide that you won't be harmed or rejected if you aren't pleasing or if you do assert yourself, this indicates that it is really safe for you to try it. What do you know about the Life Situation that makes your fear unrealistic?

_____

_____

_____

_____

Lauren's story is an example of this. Remember from Chapter 1 that Lauren was a great listener with her friends but didn't talk about herself as much as she wanted unless her friends really asked her.

In exploring her People-Pleasing Pattern, Lauren realized she expected that if she didn't please people, they wouldn't care for her and love her. In exploring the childhood origins of this, she remembered that her mother always expected Lauren to do things her way. She was withholding and distant if Lauren didn't go along with her every wish. When Lauren did please her mother, she was very loving and nurturing with Lauren. So Lauren learned that this was the only way to get love.

As Lauren thought about it, she realized that she was no longer a little girl who was dependent on her mother's love. She was a grown woman who had made it in the world. She realized that almost all of her friends would care for her and want to be close to her whether or not she went out of her way to please them. She wasn't sure about one particular friend, but she decided to practice being herself and asserting herself with her other friends, whom she knew would be supportive. She began talking about herself more when she was with her friends, whether or not they asked her first. Most of them responded well, and her connection with them improved. Lauren really enjoyed the sense of being known and cared about by her friends.

Lauren's story will be continued shortly in this chapter.

If Your Fear Is Realistic

Even though your current situation is probably not as harmful as the childhood situation that produced your underlying fears, there may be some degree of validity to your fears. If this is the case, you want to separate out those fears and perceptions that are accurate from those that are not.

If there is some validity to your fear, take a moment to get in touch with exactly what you are afraid will or won't happen if you aren't pleasing or if you are assertive. Are you afraid someone will criticize your intelligence? Are you afraid thatsomeone will lose interest in you? Write what you are afraid will happen here:

_____

_____

_____

_____

It is important to understand that you developed your relationships when you were pleasing people too much, so your friends have come to expect this from you. Therefore, it isn't surprising that some of them may have reactions when you change what they have become accustomed to. Have compassion for their feelings since they have to adjust to your change in behavior and may feel hurt at first. Explain to them clearly why you want to make this change and show them that you understand how this might be hard for them. This will go a long way toward helping them to accept your new way of relating.[6]

---

6. You may need to work on developing your Assertiveness Capacity (http://personal-growth-programs.com/people-pleasing-pattern) to succeed at this.

Creating a Plan for This Fear

Make a plan for how you will handle the situation so that either the problems related to your fear won't happen or you will protect yourself if they do.

Here are some possibilities:

1. You will assert yourself in such a way as to keep yourself from being hurt. For example, if someone tells you that your ideas are stupid, your plan will be to take a moment and think through whether or not you agree. If you don't, you will tell this person that you don't agree and explain why not.[7]

2. You will act in such a way as to maximize your chances of getting the response you want from people. For example, if you need to tell someone that you didn't like the way they treated you, you will do this in a calm way that won't trigger an angry response.

3. You will set limits that will prevent emotional harm. For example, if someone makes fun of your work, you'll tell them that ridiculing you is inappropriate and demand that they stop.[8]

4. You will sit down and talk with a person about changing their behavior so you aren't emotionally harmed or rejected. Do this at a time when you aren't in the middle of a conflict with this person. Explain how you are being hurt and make a request for the person to re-

---

7. You may need to work on developing your Assertiveness Capacity (http://personal-growth-programs.com/people-pleasing-pattern) to succeed at this.

8. You may need to work on developing your Limit-Setting Capacity (http://personal-growth-programs.com/limit-setting-capacity) for this plan to succeed.

spond differently. Volunteer to listen to their concerns as well.[9]

Work out this plan and write it here:

_____

_____

_____

_____

Then put it into operation and keep a record of your results. You may need to work through one of your patterns or develop a certain capacity for your plan to achieve the success you are looking for. Be aware that it may take time for the plan to succeed. Chapter 7 contains a practice to stop People Pleasing that involves using your plan to make this safe.

Keep in mind that your fears may be partially realistic and partially not. In that case, you will need to adopt a strategy that is a mix of these two sections.

Lauren's Relationship with Megan

As an example, let's continue with Lauren's story. Most of her friends responded well when Lauren started talking more about herself instead of just listening to them.

However, one friend, Megan, showed little interest in Lauren and kept moving the conversation back to herself. So Lauren decided to practice asserting herself with Megan.

9. You may need to work on developing your Challenge Capacity (http://personal-growth-programs.com/conflict-avoiding-pattern) and Good Communication Capacity (http://personal-growth-programs.com/blaming-pattern) to have a successful conversation.

She told Megan, "I want to talk about myself more, and I want you to be more interested in me and not keep taking all the spotlight. When I am talking about myself, you rarely ask any questions that might indicate that you really want to understand me, and you frequently change the subject back to talking about yourself."

This was a big risk, and at first Megan responded defensively.

She said, "What do you mean? I'm interested in you. I really don't know what you're talking about."

So Lauren backed down and dropped the subject.

Later when Lauren was talking to another friend about this, she realized that she had done it again. She had become compliant rather than continuing to assert herself. She realized that asserting herself once wasn't enough. She had to be able to follow through and express her needs even when the other person didn't respond well.

She decided on a plan for what to do with Megan. She brought the subject up again with her and said, "Megan, I realize that I have been overdoing my People-Pleasing thing with you for years, and now I am making big changes, so I can see how that would be hard for you. But I have been ignoring my own needs, and I don't want to do that anymore. I really want to be able to talk to you about my life and have you be interested. I know that you said you don't know what I'm talking about, and I want you to. So whenever you don't show interest in me or when you bring the conversation back to yourself, would it be OK if I point this out?" Megan looked somewhat abashed, but she agreed to this idea.

Now came the crucial work. Lauren had to actually do

it. She set an intention to notice when these problematic behaviors happened and confront Megan gently about them. The first time she did this, Megan seemed to get hurt and quiet, and Lauren was tempted to back off and not do it anymore. However, she realized that this was her Pleaser Pattern, and she vowed to keep going. She reminded herself that this would be good for Megan, too, because Megan was probably having these problems with other people as well.

As Lauren continued to point out when Megan failed to be interested in her, Megan gradually began to see what she was talking about. After a while, she admitted to Lauren, "You know, I see what you've been driving at. I do have a hard time sharing the attention with someone else. And I want to change that."

For a while, Megan made some shifts in her behavior by really asking questions about Lauren's life when Lauren was talking. Lauren was quick to praise her for this.

However, it is hard for anyone to change their behavior quickly, so there were many times when Megan reverted to her old Self-Absorbed Pattern. So Lauren had to remind herself to keep bringing it up with Megan when necessary. By this time, Lauren was feeling stronger and more powerful, so this was easier to do.

Over time, Megan did gradually change her behavior. She showed more and more interest in who Lauren was as a person and in hearing Lauren's struggles and joys in life. Lauren was finally getting what she wanted from her friendship with Megan. This ended up improving Lauren's relationship with Megan, and Lauren really enjoyed the feeling of personal power that came from asserting herself, following through, and getting what she wanted.

CHAPTER 6

The Assertiveness Capacity

Assertiveness means having a firm knowledge of what you feel, think, and desire, as opposed to being overly influenced by other people's opinions, feelings, and needs. It is part of being an autonomous adult. It also means exerting power to get what you want, stand up for yourself, protect yourself, and speak your mind. It can also mean exerting power to take care of others or to achieve what you think is right or best in a given situation. But keep in mind: Assertiveness means accomplishing these things without needing to be aggressive, controlling, judgmental, or otherwise extreme.  Assertiveness naturally integrates with cooperation, so you are open to other people's needs and opinions without giving up your own.

Aspects

❏ Knowing my feelings, opinions, and desires, even when they are different from other people's

❏ Acting according to my feelings, opinions, and desires

❐ Not being unduly influenced or controlled by other people, groups, or norms

❐ Standing up for my beliefs in the face of the other person feeling differently

❐ Initiating actions in the world

❐ Expressing my opinions, desires, and feelings

❐ Asserting power to try to bring about what I think is best in a situation

❐ Asking for what I want from other people

❐ Challenging other people when I am unhappy with something[10]

❐ Reaching out for connection without being demanding

❐ Following through when I bring something up and the other person doesn't hear me or take me seriously

❐ Staying present to my needs when I confront someone and they get hurt or defensive

❐ Saying no

❐ Setting limits on other people's harmful behavior[11]

---

10. This is related to the Challenge Capacity (http://www.personal-growth-programs.com/conflict-avoiding-pattern).
11. This is related to the Limit-Setting Capacity (http://www.personal-growth-programs.com/limit-setting-capacity).

❒ Challenging norms that are constraining

❒ Providing leadership while being open to the opinions of those I lead

❒ Challenging leadership when needed

❒ Being able to create a new subgroup or project

❒ Initiating my own work and functioning independently

❒ Other aspects_____

Lauren's Story

Remember that Lauren's boyfriend, Joe, wanted her to be more outgoing and friendly with his family. Lauren considered the question of whether Joe would still love her even if she didn't go along with everything he wanted. When she stepped back and looked at this, Lauren believed that he would, so she decided to take a risk and assert herself with Joe.

She thought about the issue that Joe had brought up about her not being outgoing and friendly enough with his family. She recognized that it was true, but there was more to it.

She said to Joe, "You know, you abandon me at family functions. You go off with your brothers and father, and don't help me to connect with your family. I need you to be with me and support me when we're with your family. Then I can get more comfortable and be able to be friendlier with them."

Joe was reluctant to do this at first because he really loved going off with the men in his family. However, Lauren practiced standing up for her needs.

She said, "Joe, this won't be forever, but I really need you to support me for the next few months with your family. Then when I feel more at ease with them, you can go off with the guys."

Joe agreed to do this, and Lauren did become more relaxed and at ease with his family over time. He was very happy about this.

Lauren continued to assert herself in other ways with Joe, and surprise, surprise! Not only did Joe not pull away from her as she had feared, but their relationship improved markedly. They were able to work through issues that had been hidden and simmering, and they ended up closer than ever.

Higher Action

In the Pattern System, in addition to healthy capacities, there are higher capacities, which are the more evolved or spiritual aspects of each capacity or dimension. When you are living from a higher capacity, you embody a version of the capacity that is less egocentric and more oriented toward  the good of the whole. You are living from a place that is informed by the sense that we are all connected, and you care for this larger unity.

The Higher Action Capacity is an integration of the higher aspects of Assertiveness and Cooperation. It has the following aspects:

Acting for the Good of the Whole

You exert influence to foster what is needed in any given situation, which means what is best for everyone, including your needs and those of everyone else. This also includes the needs of the larger whole in which you are embedded, when relevant—your family, community, cultural group, nation, and the world. This also includes the needs of those with no voice—people not present who will nevertheless be affected as well as children, animals, and the natural world. You are concerned for their higher needs—their need for growth and development, not just what would gratify them in the moment.

You recognize that you don't necessarily always know what is best in any given situation, so you work together with others to access the collective intelligence of the group in knowing what is best, and you work collectively with others to achieve this.

Which of theses aspects would you like to develop?

❐ Exerting influence for what is needed in a situation

❐ Including the needs of larger groups

❐ Including the needs of those with no voice

❐ Working for collective intelligence

❐ Taking collective action

Flexibility and Spontaneity

You are flexible in how you exert influence, depending on what is needed—sometimes being strong and forceful, sometimes soft and yielding, sometimes empowering others, sometimes being collaborative, and so on. You naturally respond with what is needed in any situation.

Which of theses aspects would you like to develop?

❐ Being flexible in the way you exert influence

❐ Naturally responding with what is needed

CHAPTER 7

Practicing Behavior Change

This chapter presents "real-time" practice where you can work on evoking your Assertiveness Capacity to replace your People-Pleasing Pattern.

This is where the rubber meets the road! This is the practice that can change your People Pleasing, and we have provided lots of support for you to make this happen, including the web workbook[12] and the People-Pleasing Online Community.[13]

Practice Outline

Here is a brief outline of the steps in this chapter:

1. Know why you want to do this practice.

2. Choose a Life Situation to practice on.

3. Know when your People Pleasing gets triggered.

4. Remind yourself that People Pleasing isn't necessary.

5. Create Assertiveness.

6. Get support for your practice.

7. Track and improve your practice.

---

12. http://www.personalgrowthapplication.com/Pattern/People PleasingWorkbook/People_Pleasing_Workbook.aspx
13. http://www.personal-growth-programs.com/connect

Clarifying Your Intention for Doing the Practice

Before you engage in this practice, it is helpful to clearly have in mind what you intend to gain by making this change. It is not enough to just decide that it would be a good thing to do. Figure out why you want to do it, set an intention for your practice, and keep this in mind during the week. This will help you discipline yourself to stick to the practice.

Think through the pain and difficulties caused by your People-Pleasing Pattern.

Notice those that will motivate you to change:

❒ I feel helpless to change the situation.

❒ I feel unsure how to express what I want.

❒ I feel oppressed by people.

❒ I feel bad about myself.

❒ My needs never get met.

❒ I feel as though I've lost myself in my relationship.

❒ Other people always come first.

❒ I don't feel powerful in my life.

❒ I feel as though I am second fiddle.

❒ I feel controlled by others.

❒ I feel inhibited from expressing my views.

❒ I feel inferior.

❒ I resent that I am not getting what I need from my relationship.

❒ Other pain and difficulties _____

_____

What do you have to gain from living from Assertiveness Capacity in your life, especially those things you really want?

☐ Growth

☐ Protection

☐ Personal power

☐ Safety

☐ Knowing myself

☐ Self-confidence

☐ Rational conversation

☐ Problem solving

☐ Getting my needs met

☐ Better self-expression

☐ A sense of equality in my relationship

☐ Other things to gain _____

_____

_____

Planning Ahead

Think of a situation that is coming up in the next week or so, or one that arises frequently, in which you want to practice the Assertiveness Capacity. Or instead, think of a situation in which you typically people please and would like to change that. For example:

• My parents keep asking when I'm going to produce a grandchild for them.

- I'm going to be invited to a coworker's wedding, and I don't want to go.

- The next time I see Aunt Marge, I know she's going to criticize me about my weight.

- My new boyfriend keeps pressuring me for sex, and I'm just not ready yet.

Let's call this the *Life Situation*. If you aren't sure when your People-Pleasing Pattern gets triggered or if it seems to be around a lot of the time, just work on noticing **whenever** that pattern is activated.

As you read through the rest of this chapter, fill in your answers here or in the web workbook. The web workbook will produce a report page that tells you what you plan to do during your life to engage in this practice. You can carry this page of the web workbook with you by printing it out or keeping it on a mobile device.

You can do this practice more than once if you want to work on more than one Life Situation. You will have a different Workbook report page for each practice. If this Life Situation isn't going to come up in the next few weeks, you can do this practice by **imagining** it coming up and how you will change your behavior.

What are you afraid of in this Life Situation? For example, if you're going to visit your parents, you might put up with their nagging about grandchildren because you're afraid they'll reject you if you stand up to them and let them know you don't want children.

You may have a few specific aspects of Assertiveness that you want to develop in this Life Situation. For example, you might want to develop your ability to speak your mind about things that upset you or to say no to tasks you don't want to take on. What aspects of Assertiveness do you want to develop in this Life Situation?

Set an intention to pay close attention during the Life Situation to see if your People-Pleasing Pattern is activated, and be prepared to practice these aspects of Assertiveness instead.

What are the feelings, thoughts, or behaviors that will cue you that your People-Pleasing Pattern is activated? For example, "It's easier to just go along," or "My needs aren't that important anyway," or "Don't make waves," or "I feel scared and small," or "I go along with my sister's demands."

Remember the target fear for this Life Situation. To the extent that it isn't true, what is true instead? What are some statements that will remind you that your target fear won't really happen or that your negative perception isn't accurate? Choose from among the following statements, or create your own:

- ❏ It is OK if I speak up and express my views.
- ❏ I don't have to think and feel as everyone else does.
- ❏ Other people aren't trying to control me.
- ❏ I won't be attacked if I assert myself.
- ❏ I won't be rejected or left if I stand up for myself.
- ❏ That person will like me more if I speak my mind.
- ❏ Most people these days like strong women.
- ❏ That person will be just fine if I assert myself.
- ❏ My friends will be happy to hear my views.

❐ Other statements _____

_____

_____

If there is some validity to your fears or perceptions, remember the plan you devised in Chapter 5 to handle that situation. You will put that plan into action this week.

Creating Assertiveness

Which of these statements will encourage you to create the aspects of Assertiveness you want in this Life Situation?

❐ I have the right to decide what actions to take for my happiness.

❐ I have my own needs and opinions.

❐ What I have to say is important.

❐ I have the right to assert what I want and make it happen.

❐ I want to share my thoughts with my partner and friends.

❐ I am strong, grounded, and intelligent.

❐ I do not have to be exactly like everyone else.

❐ If I assert myself, people will still like me.

❐ I am more interesting if I assert myself.

❐ I am an independent thinker who considers other people's feelings.

❐ Other statements _____

_____

_____

You can develop an aspect of yourself that I call the Inner Champion, which supports you in being yourself and feeling good about yourself despite your fears. Your Assertiveness Inner Champion encourages you to feel confident in your ability to speak up on your own behalf without fear.

Visit http://www.personalgrowthapplication.com/ Pattern/PeoplePleasingWorkbook/People_Pleasing_ Workbook_Meditation.aspx to do a guided meditation to access your Assertiveness Inner Champion.

Which of the following statements would you like your Assertiveness Inner Champion to say to you?

- ❐ You have the right to get what you want.
- ❐ You have the right to your opinions.
- ❐ Your feelings are unique to you. No one can tell you what to feel.
- ❐ You have the right to take charge of your life.
- ❐ You can exert power without fear.

❐ You can say no whenever you want.

❐ You have the right to stand up for yourself.

❐ You can speak your mind.

❐ Your thoughts are just as valid as anyone else's.

❐ Your needs are just as important as other people's.

❐ Other statements _____

_____

_____

What body sensation, feeling, or state of consciousness will help you evoke these aspects of Assertiveness (for example, that sense of inner strength when you speak up for yourself)? _____

_____

_____

What image will help create Assertiveness (for example, a women's soccer player celebrating)? _____

_____

_____

Can any people close to you help you create Assertiveness? What help do you want from them (for example, to remind you that you have a right to your own preferences)?

_____

_____

_____

Is there something you want people close to you to stop doing (for example, appreciating how flexible and accommodating you are)? _____

_____

_____

Talk to the people close to you about what they can do (or stop doing) that will help you activate the Assertiveness Capacity and especially the aspects of Assertiveness you want in this Life Situation.

Your Assertiveness Practice Workbook Section

There is a separate section of the web workbook for helping you engage in your Assertiveness Practice and keep track of it. The rest of this chapter explains how to engage in this practice and use this section.

Working with a Buddy

People have much more success with practices like this if they have a "buddy" to witness them and be their cheerleader. I recommend that you find a friend who is a good listener and who will understand what you are doing and be supportive. Or join our People-Pleasing Online Community,[14] where we will help you find a buddy.

After you make your plans for the practice, call your buddy and talk through what you will be doing. If you have written down specific words you want to say in the situation, practice saying them to your buddy. Even role-play the situation. For example, have your buddy play your lover while you practice expressing a strong preference.

Set a time frame for checking in with your buddy on your progress with the practice. You could just do it once at the end of a week to report on how the practice has gone. But for even more effective support, consider checking in with your buddy every two or three days, or even every day, to let him or her know how it is going. The act of reporting in will really help to keep you on track. When you know that you'll be talking to someone about your practice, you'll be much more likely to do it and to keep track of what happened.

Your buddy can also support you in speaking up in situations in which you have "just gone along" in the past. You can share those situations with your buddy, knowing that you will be talking to him or her about whether or not you spoke up on your own behalf. This can be crucial support for being accountable for your action plans and following through on them.

---

14. http://www.personal-growth-programs.com/connect

When the Life Situation Occurs

With some Life Situations, you know ahead of time when they will happen. For example, you know when you will be preparing to ask for a raise. In these cases, take some time right before this happens to go to Assertiveness Practice Plans[15] in the web workbook (or review the pages in the paperback workbook) to review how you want to handle this Life Situation. (Keep in mind that the web workbook and the Profile Program are two different programs.) If you don't have time right before it happens, take some time earlier to prepare.

Some situations allow you to process this material **during** the Life Situation. For example, if the Life Situation involves responding to a request from a family member, you can say you need to think about your answer. After you take a time-out to process the People-Pleasing feelings that are coming up, you can resume the conversation and put your plan into operation. In this case, when you take the time-out, click the above two links to review how you plan to handle the situation so you can decide what to do.

During the Life Situation, pay close attention and notice the feelings, thoughts, or behavior that will cue you that your People-Pleasing Pattern is activated.

If it is triggered, do the following:

- Say the statements (out loud or silently) that will remind you that you don't have to be afraid of Assertiveness, or create your own on the spot.

---

15. http://personalgrowthapplication.com/Pattern/PeoplePleasing Workbook/People_Pleasing_Workbook_Practice_Plans.aspx?pname= LifeSituation

- Put your plan into action to assert yourself around the possibility of harm or rejection.

- Say the statements (out loud or silently) that will inspire you to create Assertiveness, or create your own on the spot.

- Use a body sensation, feeling, or state of consciousness (if you have chosen one) to help create Assertiveness.

- Look at the image you have chosen (if you have one) to inspire you to create Assertiveness.

If you were successful in creating Assertiveness, celebrate your success! Give yourself a pat on the back or a reward, such as a nature hike. Appreciate yourself for this step in changing your behavior. It is very important to reinforce each step, however small, in the right direction. Your Assertiveness Practice Workbook will help you in rewarding your steps toward success.

After the situation has happened, enter your Practice Notes (see below) as soon as you have time to enter what happened. Or if you don't have time, do it at the end of the day when doing your Daily Check-In Notes.

If you came up with new statements, add them to your workbook to use in the future. If you have additional insights into any of the material you have filled out previously in the workbook, feel free to add them to the pages you have already filled out.

Practice Notes

Enter your answers according to what you did in your practice. (Not all need to be answered.)

The Life Situation _____

_____

_____

The fears that came up in this situation _____

_____

_____

The aspects of Assertiveness you were working on developing in this situation _____

_____

_____

What triggered the People-Pleasing Pattern _____

_____

_____

The statements you said to remind yourself that you don't have to be afraid of Assertiveness _____

_____

_____

_____

What you did to assert yourself to handle harm or rejection _____

_____

_____

_____

The statements you said to yourself to inspire you to create Assertiveness _____

_____

_____

The body sensation, feeling, or state of consciousness you used to help create Assertiveness _____

_____

_____

The image you used to inspire you to create Assertiveness

_____

_____

How you did in attempting to create Assertiveness

_____

_____

_____

Further notes on what happened _____

_____

_____

_____

Is there anything you want to do differently next time?

_____

_____

_____

Daily Check-In

In order to remember to do this practice, it will help you to check in with yourself once a day in addition to any checking in with your friend. Choose a time when you will have a few minutes to yourself and when it will be easy for you to remember to check in each day. For many people, this is right before going to bed each night or upon waking each morning. But in all cases, choose a consistent time of day that works best for you.

If the Life Situation only occurs once a week or a few times a month, you don't need to enter Daily Check-In Notes every day. Just reflect to see if it happened that day and take notes if it did. On the days it didn't happen, you don't need to do anything.

Take notes on what you were aware of that day. If the Life Situation occurred, write down what happened. Enter your notes below.

Reflect on whether the People-Pleasing Pattern was activated today, whether you noticed and did the practice, and what happened. _____

_____

_____

Did the Life Situation happen today? _____

_____

_____

If so, were you paying attention when it happened? _____

_____

Did the People-Pleasing Pattern get triggered today (in that situation or any other one)? _____

If so, did you notice when the People-Pleasing Pattern was triggered today? _____

If you didn't, what kept you from noticing? _____

_____

_____

_____

What can you do tomorrow to help you be more aware?

_____

_____

_____

If you did notice that the People-Pleasing Pattern was triggered, did you do the practice to evoke Assertiveness?

_____

If not, what stopped you from doing that? _____

_____

_____

What can you do next time to help yourself remember to evoke Assertiveness? _____

_____

_____

If you did the practice and didn't track what happened at the time, enter it under Practice Notes. If you did it more than once, take separate notes for each instance by clicking that link multiple times.

Is there anything you want to do differently tomorrow or the next time your People-Pleasing Pattern is triggered?

_____

_____

_____

Weekly Check-In

After a week, take notes on how this practice is working.

Day of week _____

How many times did you do the practice this week? _____

Was this enough to be helpful to you? _____

If you did the practice enough, how much of a difference did it make? _____

_____

What worked in doing the practice? _____

_____

_____

_____

What didn't work in doing the practice? _____

_____

_____

_____

Do you want to do the practice again next week? _____

Is there anything you want to do differently next week?

_____

_____

_____

CHAPTER 8

The Power Dimension

The information in this chapter will help you to get a fuller sense of the various patterns and healthy capacities that you might have with respect to Assertiveness. You might learn about other patterns you want to explore and may see the relationships between your patterns and capacities. However, if you aren't interested in this level of complexity, feel free to skip this chapter or come back to it at a later time.

The Power Dimension

The People-Pleasing Pattern is part of the *Power Dimension* in the Pattern System. Let's look at how it is related to the other patterns and capacities.

There are four problematic patterns in the Power Dimension—People Pleasing, Passive-Aggressive, Controlling, and Defiant.

- The **People-Pleasing Pattern** involves complying with what other people want and trying to make them happy.

- The **Passive-Aggressive Pattern** involves outwardly attempting to please people while rebelling against them in subtle ways that leave them frustrated and confused.

- The **Controlling Pattern** involves being dominant and demanding, and expecting to have things your way.

- The **Defiant Pattern** involves rebelling against other people's power in an attempt to preserve your autonomy.

Two healthy capacities—Cooperation and Assertiveness—are related to these four patterns.

- **Cooperation** is the ability to be receptive and work well with others.

- **Assertiveness**, as discussed previously, is the ability to think and act for yourself and to exert power to get what you want, protect yourself, or achieve what you think is right.

Cooperation is a complement to Assertiveness. For healthy relating, you need capacities on both sides. Cooperation helps you to work with people in a connected way, and Assertiveness helps you express yourself and your personal power.

This is the nature of healthy capacities—they naturally integrate with each other, which means that they don't oppose each other. They work together; they both support your flourishing in power-related areas of your life. If you have both capacities, you are able to work in harmony with others while at the same time think for yourself and speak up on your own behalf.

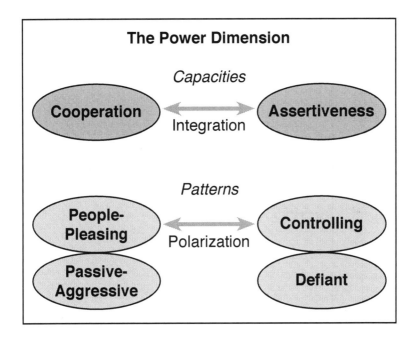

Relations Between the Patterns and Capacities

Patterns in Conflict

The patterns on the left and right sides don't integrate with each other in the way the healthy capacities do. They are polarized, which means they battle each other to determine how you relate to others. The People-Pleasing and Passive-Aggressive Patterns involve giving away your power or appearing to do so. In contrast, the Controlling and Defiant Patterns involve attempts to have too much power. Another way to look at it is that the patterns on the left are about *under*functioning, while the two on the right are about *over*functioning.

Patterns Are Dysfunctional Versions of Capacities

Cooperation is a healthy version of People Pleasing or Passive-Aggression. Another way to say this is that People Pleasing and Passive-Aggression are extreme, dysfunctional versions of Cooperation. It is an attempt to be cooperative by giving yourself up. And the same applies on the right side. Assertiveness is a healthy version of Control and Defiance. Or you can say that those two are extreme, dysfunctional versions of Assertiveness.

Capacities Resolve Patterns

If you have a People-Pleasing or Passive-Aggressive Pattern, Assertiveness is what you need to develop to break away from it. That is why Assertiveness is emphasized in this book on People Pleasing. Thus the capacity on the opposite side of the graphic is the one needed to break from a pattern. In order to get there, you will need the courage to face and work through your fears, develop confidence in your right to your own thoughts and opinions, and practice speaking up for yourself regularly.

The same applies on the other side. If you have a Controlling or Defiant Pattern, you need to develop Cooperation to break away from it.

Here is another graphic showing these relationships:

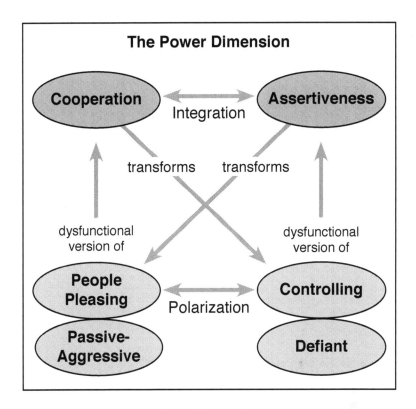

Questionnaire

It would be helpful to track which of the patterns and capacities in this dimension you have. You may have an idea from reading the descriptions, or you can take a quiz on my website. This questionnaire will give you a score for each of the patterns and capacities in the Power Dimension to help clarify how strongly you have the People-Pleasing Pattern or each of the other patterns in that dimension. It will also tell you how high you score on the healthy capacities in that dimension. To take this quiz, visit http://www.personalgrowthapplication.com/Members/Questionnaire.aspx?Questionnaire=6.

CHAPTER 9

Conclusion

Deep Healing and Transformation
of the People-Pleasing Pattern

When I do psychotherapy with my clients, I use Internal Family Systems Therapy (IFS), a very powerful, cutting-edge approach developed by pioneering psychologist Richard Schwartz, PhD. Since I discovered IFS a decade ago, I have seen amazing results in my clients' lives. I was developing the Pattern System for more than a decade before I discovered IFS and was thrilled to find that the two are a natural fit.

IFS work can complement the work you do on your People-Pleasing Pattern using this book. IFS would help you to experientially access the motivations and childhood origins behind this pattern and to heal and transform the pattern. Then your homework practice on developing your Assertiveness Capacity would be even more effective. If you want to experience the most profound and lasting change in your pattern, I recommend that you practice IFS with your People-Pleasing Part as described below.

The IFS Model

IFS enables you to understand each of the *parts* of your psyche, sometimes called *subpersonalities*. Think of them as little people inside you. Each has its own perspective, feelings, memories, goals, and motivations. And sometimes they are at odds with each other. For example, one part of you might be trying to lose weight, and another part might want to eat whatever you want. We all have many different parts, such as the procrastinator, the lover, the inner critic, the lonely child, the rebel, the caretaker, and so on.

If you have the People-Pleasing Pattern, there is a part of you that tries to please other people and make them happy, at your own expense. You can use IFS to work on your People-Pleasing Part as well as any other patterns you have.

IFS recognizes that we all have child parts that are in pain, which are called *exiles*. These correspond to the wounds in the Pattern System. The parts that try to keep us from feeling this pain are called *protectors*, which correspond to the patterns.

Most important, IFS recognizes that we all have a true *Self*, which is our core healthy place or spiritual center. IFS has some innovative and easy ways to access Self. You get to know your parts and develop trusting relationships with them from the place of Self, which then leads to healing and transformation of those parts.

The IFS Process with Your People-Pleasing Part

IFS is an experiential therapy. You don't just get insight into your parts—you actually go inside, contact them, and have conversations with them.

What follows is a brief description of how you would do IFS with your People-Pleasing Part. It is just an overview to give you an idea of how the process works. The actual procedure is much more detailed and specialized. We don't expect you to be able to do IFS by reading this brief description. You will need to learn how to engage in the IFS process using my book *Self-Therapy* or courses, or by going into individual therapy with an IFS therapist (see Appendix C).

First you access your People-Pleasing Part experientially. You might feel it emotionally, or hear its words, or get a mental image of what it looks like. Then you access Self so that you are separate from your People-Pleasing Part and have a place to stand from which to connect with it. You make sure that you are open to getting to know it from its own perspective rather than judging it or wanting to get rid of it.

Then you ask it to tell you what it is trying to accomplish for you by keeping you focused on trying to please other people. You want to know what it is afraid would happen if it allowed you to speak up on your own behalf. This helps you to recognize the exile (wounded inner child part) that it is protecting.

This conversation will give you a good sense of how the People-Pleasing Part is trying to protect you, even if that protection isn't really needed anymore. This allows you to appreciate its efforts on your behalf, and your appreciation helps the People-Pleasing Part to trust you.

You ask the People-Pleasing Part for permission to work with the exile it is protecting. Then you get to know that child part and find out what happened when you were young to cause that part to be so afraid and wounded. You witness these memories in an experiential way (you may or may not know them already)—that is, you see them in a mental movie of your past. Then you enter the childhood scene and give that little child what he or she needed back then, or you protect the wounded child part from being harmed. You might also take that part out of that harmful or painful childhood situation and into your present life, where he or she will be safe and can be connected to you and receive your love and caring.

You help the exile to release the pain and fear that he or she has been carrying all these years. Once this is done, your People-Pleasing Part won't feel the need to protect the exile anymore, so it can now relax and stop trying please others while ignoring your own needs. Then you will be able to pay attention to your needs and speak up for yourself as you want.

My book *Self-Therapy* describes in detail how to use IFS to work through any psychological issue. See <u>www.selfleader ship.org</u> for detailed information about IFS and professional training in the Model. My colleagues and I also offer courses in which you can learn how to use IFS to work on yourself and do peer counseling with other people from the course. See Appendix C for IFS resources.

Conclusion

I hope this book will help you to transform your People-Pleasing Pattern so you can have the assertiveness, autonomy, and personal power that you desire. In order for this to happen, it is important that you fully engage in the practice of creating Assertiveness in Chapter 7. Reading this material and understanding yourself is an important step, but most people need to consciously work on putting this into practice in their lives.

You also may need to work on other patterns of yours in order to fully let go of People Pleasing. Your People-Pleasing Pattern may be linked to a Dependent Pattern, a Conflict-

Avoiding Pattern, or one of the others that are mentioned in the book. You may be able to create the Assertiveness you want by only focusing on your People-Pleasing Pattern, but you might need to do more to achieve success. If this is the case, read other books in this series, or use the web application when it becomes available, or find other ways to work on those patterns.

Don't become discouraged if your pattern doesn't transform right away. Personal growth isn't a simple, easy process, despite what some self-help books would have you believe. Letting go of a deep-seated problem takes time and effort and a commitment to work on yourself.

Personal growth is an exciting journey, with twists and turns, painful revelations, unexpected insights, profound shifts, and an ever-deepening sense of self-awareness and mastery. I hope that this book contributes to your personal evolution and the deep satisfaction that comes from feeling powerful in your world.

The Pattern System^{SM}

The People-Pleasing Pattern and the Power Dimension that contains it are just one small part of the overall Pattern System. You can use the Pattern System to obtain a complete map of your psyche. You will be able to see your strengths and your defenses, your places of pain and how you compensate for them. You'll come to understand the structure of your inner conflicts and see where you are ready to grow. The Pattern System makes clear what you need to explore next in order to resolve the issues that are most important to you.

The goal of working with the Pattern System is to live from your True Self, which is who you naturally are when you aren't operating from patterns and when you have developed skills for healthy relating and functioning. Assertiveness is one aspect of the True Self.

A more advanced goal is to live from your Higher Self, which is your spiritual ground and is the integration of the higher capacities, including Higher Action.

Interpersonal Dimensions in the Pattern System

The Power Dimension is just one of ten interpersonal dimensions in the Pattern System, each containing at least two patterns and two capacities. The following are brief descriptions of some of them:

Conflict. How do you deal with differences of opinion as well as desires, disagreements, judgment, anger, and fights? Do you use avoidance tactics? Do you become angry, blaming, or defensive? Can you communicate your concerns without judgment and own your part in a problem? Do you become frightened or feel bad about yourself? Can you bring up conflicts and set limits on attacks?

Social. How do you relate to people socially? Are you outgoing or shy, scared or confident in reaching out to people or making conversation? Are you self-effacing or charming, attention seeking or avoiding? Are you overly oriented toward performance in the way you relate to others, or are you more genuine?

Care. How do you balance your needs vs. other people's needs? Do you end up taking care of others rather than yourself? Do people tell you that you don't show enough care or concern for them?

Intimacy. Do you avoid intimacy, need it too much, fear it, love it? Can you be autonomous in an intimate relationship without denying your needs? Do you get overly dependent in relationships, or can you support yourself?

Power. How do you deal with power in your relationships? Do you give in too easily to others or try too hard to please them? Do you need to be in control? Do you feel as though you must stand up for yourself against people you view as dominating? Do you frustrate others without realizing why? Can you assert yourself? Can you work with people in a spirit of cooperation?

Anger and Strength. How do you deal with self-protection and assertiveness in situations that can bring up anger?

Do you dump your anger on people? Do you disown your anger and therefore lose your strength? Can you be centered and communicate clearly when you are angry? Can you be strong and forceful without being reactive?

Trust. Are you usually trusting of people, or do you easily get suspicious? Can you perceive when someone isn't trustworthy, or are you gullible?

Some additional interpersonal dimensions are:

- Honesty
- Evaluation
- Responsibility

Each of these dimensions has the same structure as the Power Dimension.

The following is a chart of all ten interpersonal dimensions and their patterns and capacities. There are two types of patterns—hard and soft. The *Hard Patterns* (on the right side) tend to be aggressive and cause other people pain, while the *Soft Patterns* (on the left side) tend to be passive and cause the person pain. If you have a Hard Pattern, you need to develop the corresponding capacity on the left side, which is a Relational Capacity. If you have a Soft Pattern, you need to develop the corresponding capacity on the right side, which is a Self-Supporting Capacity. This is, of course, just a quick summary; the interpersonal patterns will be explained in detail in a future book.

The Interpersonal Dimensions of the Pattern System℠

Jay Earley, PhD

Soft Patterns	*Relational Capacities*	DIMENSION	*Self-Supporting Capacities*	Hard Patterns
		RECEPTIVE ← → ACTIVE		
Dependent	*Intimacy*	**INTIMACY**	*Self-Support*	Distancing
Conflict-Avoiding	*Good Communication*	**CONFLICT**	*Challenge, Limit Setting*	Blaming, Defensive
People-Pleasing, Passive-Aggressive	*Cooperation*	**POWER**	*Assertiveness*	Controlling, Defiant
Caretaking	*Caring*	**CARE**	*Self-Care*	Self-Absorbed, Entitled
Self-Effacing	*Genuineness*	**SOCIAL**	*Social Confidence*	Charmer
Disowned Anger	*Centeredness*	**STRENGTH**	*Strength*	Angry
Gullible	*Trust*	**TRUST**	*Perceptiveness*	Suspicious
Deceptive	*Tact*	**HONESTY**	*Honesty*	Judgmental
Idealizing	*Appreciation*	**EVALUATION**	*Perceptiveness*	Judgmental
Victim, Powerless	*Vulnerability*	**RESPONSIBILITY**	*Responsibility*	Controlling

There will be a book on each of the interpersonal patterns. Visit http://personal-growth-programs.com/pattern-sys tem/pattern-system-series to see which ones are available now.

Personal Dimensions in the Pattern System

The Pattern System also deals with a variety of personal patterns. The following are brief descriptions of some of them:

Self-Esteem. Do you feel good about yourself, or do you constantly judge yourself? Do you accept yourself as you are? Do you try to prop up your self-esteem with pride? How do you deal with improving yourself?

Accomplishment. Are you confident in working on and accomplishing tasks? Do you procrastinate? Do you push or judge yourself to try to get things done or to achieve, or can you accomplish with ease?

Pleasure. How do you deal with food, drink, sex, and other bodily pleasures? Do you indulge in harmful ways? Do you control yourself rigidly to avoid doing that? Do you bounce back and forth between overindulging and castigating yourself for that?

Some further personal dimensions are:

- Action
- Change
- Hope
- Excellence
- Decision
- Risk
- Rationality/Emotion

Each of these dimensions has the same structure as the Power Dimension. There will be a book on each of the patterns in each dimension. Visit http://personal-growth-programs.com/pattern-system/pattern-system-series to see which ones are available now.

Wounds

The following are the main wounds:

Deficit Wounds

1. Deprivation Wound

2. Abandonment Wound

3. Rejection Wound

4. Not Seen Wound

Harm Wounds

1. Judgment Wound

2. Shame Wound

3. Domination Wound

4. Guilt Wound

5. Violation Wound

6. Attack Wound

7. Betrayal Wound

8. Exploitation Wound

Deficiency Wounds

1. Unlovable Wound

2. Inadequate Wound

3. Depressed Wound

4. Basic Deficiency Wound

Motivations

The following are some of the important motivations:

- Fear of Harm
- Fear of Rejection
- Fear of Losing Yourself
- Attempt to Stop Harm
- Attempt to Stop Pain
- Attempt to Get Connection
- Fear of Success
- Fear of Failure
- Opposition to a Parent

An Open-Ended System

The Pattern System is open-ended. We sometimes add new patterns, subpatterns, capacities, and dimensions, or even new types of patterns. We welcome input from other people in developing the Pattern System further. See http:// thepatternsystem.wikispaces.com for a fuller outline of the system.

Definitions of Terms

Dimension. An area of psychological functioning (e.g., power, intimacy, or self-esteem) that contains certain patterns and capacities that deal with similar issues.

Healthy Capacity. A way of behaving or feeling that makes your life productive, connected, and happy. An aspect of the True Self.

Higher Self. Your spiritual ground and the integration of your higher capacities.

Inner Champion. An aspect of yourself that supports and encourages you and helps you feel good about yourself. It is the magic bullet for dealing with the negative impact of the Inner Critic.

Inner Critic. A part of you that judges you, demeans you, and pushes you to do things. It tends to make you feel bad about yourself.

Interpersonal Pattern. A pattern that involves interpersonal relating.

Life Situation. A situation that is coming up in the next week or two in which you will have the opportunity to practice creating a healthy capacity instead of prolonging a pattern.

Motivation. A kind of underlying intention (e.g., fear of harm or desire for approval) that drives a pattern.

Pattern. A way of behaving or feeling that is a problem for you or others (e.g., being dependent, controlling, or judgmental). A pattern tends to be too rigid, extreme, dysfunctional, or inappropriate for the situation you are in.

Polarization. A dynamic in which two patterns are fighting each other to determine how you behave or relate to others.

True Self. Who you naturally are when you aren't operating from patterns and when you have developed skills for healthy relating and functioning. The healthy capacities are aspects of the True Self.

Wound. A harmful or traumatic way you were treated, usually in childhood (e.g., being neglected, hit, or dismissed).

APPENDIX C

Resources

Books

Self-Therapy, by Jay Earley. How to do Internal Family Systems (IFS) sessions on your own or with a partner. Also a manual of the IFS method that can be used by therapists.

Self-Therapy for Your Inner Critic, by Jay Earley and Bonnie Weiss. Applies IFS to working with Inner Critic parts.

Resolving Inner Conflict, by Jay Earley. How to work with polarization using IFS.

Working with Anger in IFS, by Jay Earley. How to work with too much anger or disowned anger using IFS.

Activating Your Inner Champion Instead of Your Inner Critic, by Jay Earley and Bonnie Weiss. How to bring forth your Inner Champion to deal with attacks from your Inner Critic.

Embracing Intimacy, by Jay Earley. How to work through blocks that keep you from having the intimacy you want in your love relationship.

Letting Go of Perfectionism, by Jay Earley and Bonnie Weiss. How to work through fears that lead to perfectionism so you can have more ease and perspective in your life.

Taking Action, by Jay Earley. How to work through procrastination and achieve your goals.

A series of Pattern System books similar to this one will be published over the next few years. A list of the currently available Pattern System books will be maintained and updated at http://www.personal-growth-programs.com/pattern-system-series.

Updates for this book. Visit http://www.personal-growth-programs.com/a-pleaser-no-longer-owners to register yourself as an owner of this book. You will receive an updated version of the ebook whenever it is improved. You will also be notified about each new book in the series as it comes out.

Courses

My colleagues and I teach telephone courses on perfectionism, procrastination, and many of the other topics of the Pattern System books. We also teach telephone courses on IFS for the general public. My website (with Bonnie Weiss) http://www.personal-growth-programs.com has the details.

Websites and Applications

My IFS website (with Bonnie Weiss), http://www.personal-growth-programs.com, contains popular and professional articles on IFS and its application to various psychological issues. You can also sign up for our email list to receive future articles and notifications of upcoming courses and groups.

My personal website, http://www.jayearley.com, contains more of my writings and information about my psychotherapy practice, including my therapy groups.

Our other website, http://www.psychemaps.com, contains a questionnaire to determine which of the seven types of Inner Critics you have and a program to profile your Inner Critic and Inner Champion.

The People-Pleasing Online Community (http://www.personal-growth-programs.com/connect) is for people who are reading this book and would like to support each other in letting go of People Pleasing. It is part of a larger online community of people who are working on various aspects of their personal growth and healing through our books, websites, and programs.

The Pattern System website, http://thepatternsystem.wikispaces.com, contains an outline of the latest version.

I am also developing a web application based on the Pattern System and IFS that will allow people to explore their psychological issues and do self-therapy.

The Center for Self-Leadership is the official IFS organization. Its website, http://www.selfleadership.org, contains IFS articles, trainings, workshops, and a list of IFS therapists.

Books and Booklets by
Jay Earley, PhD

The IFS Series
Self-Therapy

Self-Therapy for Your Inner Critic (with Bonnie Weiss)

Resolving Inner Conflict

Working with Anger in IFS

Negotiating for Self-Leadership**

The Pattern System Series
Embracing Intimacy

Letting Go of Perfectionism (with Bonnie Weiss)

Taking Action: Working Through Procrastination
and Achieving Your Goals

A Pleaser No Longer

Beyond Caretaking**

The Inner Critic Series (with Bonnie Weiss)
Self-Therapy for Your Inner Critic

Activating Your Inner Champion
in Place of Your Inner Critic

Letting Go of Perfectionism

Other Books
Interactive Group Therapy

Transforming Human Culture

Inner Journeys

**Forthcoming

Printed in Great Britain
by Amazon